To: Dayton
From: Matä

the **enlightened kitchen**

the **enlightened kitchen**

Fresh Vegetable Dishes from the Temples of Japan

Mari Fujii

Photographs by **Tae Hamamura**

Translation by **Richard Jeffery**

KODANSHA INTERNATIONAL
Tokyo • New York • London

The author and publisher would like to give special thanks to the following companies
for their contribution to the production of this book:
Sanada Ltd., who provided the dried ingredients used in recipes and photographs.
Wasalaby, who loaned their exquisite Japanese tableware for use in the photographs.

Distributed in the United States by Kodansha America, Inc., and in
the United Kingdom and continental Europe by Kodansha Europe Ltd.

Published by Kodansha International Ltd., 17-14 Otowa 1-chome,
Bunkyo-ku, Tokyo 112-8652, and Kodansha America, Inc.

First edition, 2005
15 14 13 12 11 10 09 08 07 06 05   10 9 8 7 6 5 4 3 2 1

www.kodansha-intl.com

CONTENTS

INTRODUCTION

The Enlightened Kitchen

The vegetarian food eaten by monks and nuns in Japan's Buddhist temples is known as "shojin ryori," or "shojin cuisine." This traditional temple cuisine uses no animal products. All ingredients come from plant sources, such as vegetables, seaweed, wild plants, grains and pulses, in the belief that this way of eating has numerous physical and spiritual benefits.

I have been teaching people how to make temple food for over twenty years, with my husband Sotetsu, who is a Buddhist priest. At our temple in the old seaside town of Kamakura, near Tokyo, we host many foreign visitors who come to us to learn about the magic of temple cuisine. Whether from America, Europe or Asia, all agree that temple food is light on the stomach yet satisfying enough to see them through to the next mealtime. This traditional way of eating is also seeing a surge in popularity among Japanese people. What is it about temple cuisine that appeals so widely?

A Natural Cuisine

These days, hothouse cultivation methods mean that that many vegetables are grown year round, irrespective of the season. In Japan, you can find pumpkins imported from the southern hemisphere in the supermarket in winter. Nobody seems to know a vegetable's true season any more. How things have changed since I was a child fifty years ago! In those days, we only ate freshly harvested seasonal vegetables. Since no green vegetables grew in winter, we would preserve them in the fall and eat them pickled throughout the cold months.

Temple cuisine uses seasonal ingredients in the belief that following the flow of nature is best for the body. Eating food in season provides your body with the nourishment it needs at a given time of year. The slight bitterness of spring buds and shoots, for example, is said to remove the fat the body accumulates during winter. Summer vegetables from the melon family, such as tomatoes, eggplants and cucumbers, have a cooling effect on the body. Fall provides an abundant harvest of sweet potatoes, yams, pumpkins, chestnuts and fruit, which revive tired bodies after the heat of summer. In winter, a variety of root vegetables, such as daikon radish, turnip, and lotus root provide warmth and sustenance.

A Creative Cuisine

When vegetables are seasonal there is often a glut of a particular ingredient at a particular time of year. A variety of cooking methods (frying, boiling, grilling) and seasoning (spices, salt, miso, soy sauce) allows the same vegetable to be enjoyed in many different ways. When cooking with daikon radish, for example, the skin can be sliced thinly and fried, the root can be boiled, and the leaves can be blanched, finely chopped, and mixed with rice. Leftover boiled daikon can be enjoyed the next day—perhaps dipped in batter and deep-fried. Studying the ingredients and the various ways of cooking them is an important part of temple cuisine, and it allows the originality of the cook to come to the fore. This way of eating, in which the whole foodstuff is used, without wasting any of it, is also kind to the environment.

A Healthy Cuisine

In addition to seasonal vegetables, dried foodstuffs such as seaweed, shiitake mushrooms, and the tofu products yuba and koyadofu are often used in temple cuisine. These sun-dried ingredients, with their high nutritional value and concentrated flavor, are traditional staples in the Japanese diet.

Eating dried foodstuffs is said to ensure a long, healthy life. Seaweed, for example, is rich in fiber, calcium, minerals, and iodine, and is known to control blood pressure and cholesterol levels. Tofu products are high in protein yet low in calories and fat. I heartily recommend that you make these traditional Japanese dried foodstuffs part of your everyday grocery cupboard.

Artificial flavorings are never used in temple cuisine. Salt, soy sauce, mirin, and miso are the basic seasonings. Fragrance is added to dishes with ingredients such as the winter citrus fruit yuzu, the herbs sansho and shiso, and sesame oil. Sugar is rarely used, although bearing in mind that mirin may be hard to find, I have suggested sugar or maple syrup as a substitute in some recipes. Seasoning is generally kept light, however, the better to enjoy the delicious natural flavor of fresh vegetables. On my visits to various regions of Japan, where I have cooked using freshly harvested local produce, I always find that vegetables are perfectly delicious eaten on their own, with just a little seasoning. In fact, people who sample my cooking are often astonished to find just how sweet the natural flavor of vegetables can be.

Nutritious, low-calorie temple cuisine is the perfect antidote to the unhealthy eating habits of today's society, where processed, additive-laden foods are the norm, and diet-related disorders such as diabetes and high blood pressure are widespread.

A Buddhist Cuisine

My husband Sotetsu spent ten years living as a monk in various Buddhist temples, following a strict regime of personal and spiritual discipline. In addition to spiritual training, there are a number of practical jobs monks have to carry out to ensure the smooth day-to-day running of the temple, such as accountant, secretary to the chief abbot, and tenzo, or temple cook, a job which always fell to my husband.

The basic meal in a Buddhist temple consists of one soup, one side dish, and a bowl of rice. More elaborate meals are served when there are guests, or for special occasions such as New Year or other feast days. The number of dishes increase, and will perhaps include red-bean rice or udon noodles. In line with the Buddhist precept that forbids the killing of living things "that flee when chased," the eating of meat and fish is not allowed. Strong smelling vegetables such as leeks, scallions, garlic and onions, which are believed to promote sexual energy, and alcohol, which clouds the mind, are also prohibited as these would disrupt the monks' training. Saké, however, is sometimes used as a seasoning.

The tenzo prepares the ingredients and cooks the meals, but there is more to his job than this. Mealtimes offer the monks the only moments of relief in a day filled with monotonous training. The meal has to be a heart-warming affair. My husband always says that seeing the happy faces of the monks as they ate his food made him feel that his job was worthwhile.

When my husband was training as tenzo, he was told by his master to "pour the spirit of heaven and earth into every dish." Even a meal that consists of one simple dish can be made with care and attention. Thinking of the people who will eat the food you make, and cooking with your whole heart will affect all other parts of your daily life. In other words, carrying out ordinary chores earnestly is good spiritual practice for everyone. In the midst of life's daily rush, take the time to perform daily tasks mindfully, including the preparation of food. At mealtimes, savor the food slowly, while appreciating the work of the cook.

I have selected recipes that are easy to make at home with readily obtainable ingredients. Without straying too far from the original flavor of temple food, I have included many suggestions for enhancing the dishes with various seasonings and herbs. Although Japanese temple food is strictly plant-based, in China and Tibet, from where Buddhist cuisine was first imported to Japan, dairy products are traditionally used, and some of my recipes contain yogurt or cheese.

Perhaps the key to fully appreciating temple cuisine is to select and prepare ingredients with care, and to eat with relaxed enjoyment. People often say that they feel that a weight has lifted from their shoulders after eating temple food. One writer who came to visit us called temple cuisine "soul food." It seems that something in this simple, traditional cuisine touches people's hearts. It is my sincere hope that both your heart and your body will reap the benefits of this soothing, healthful way of cooking and eating.

Mari Fujii

SOUP

Deep-Fried Lotus Root Soup

Crispy balls of deep-fried lotus root add crunch and texture to the rich taste of this konbu-flavored soup. Serve piping hot.

serves 4

1 pound 2 ounces (500 g) lotus root, peeled and finely grated

2 teaspoons cornstarch

vegetable oil, for deep-frying

3 1/3 cups (800 ml) konbu stock (see page 98)

2 tablespoons soy sauce

1/4 teaspoon salt

2 tablespoons saké

4 or 5 stalks mitsuba or baby spinach, for garnish, optional

1. Place the grated lotus root in a colander to drain.

2. In a bowl, mix the lotus root and cornstarch, then form into about 12 bite-sized balls.

3. Heat the vegetable oil to 340–360°F (170–180°C). Deep-fry the lotus-root balls until they turn golden brown.

4. Place the konbu stock, soy sauce, salt, and saké in a saucepan, and bring to a boil.

5. Divide the lotus-root balls between individual soup bowls, cover with the konbu stock, and garnish with mitsuba sprigs.

Lotus root turns a darker color after being sliced. Once sliced, it should be cooked immediately, or kept fresh in a bowl of water to which a few drops of vinegar have been added.

Kenchin Style Vegetable Soup

Originally from Kenchoji Temple, the first Zen Buddhist temple in Japan, this warming soup is a typical temple dish, made from root vegetables stir-fried in sesame oil then simmered in konbu-flavored broth. Crumbling a block of tofu into the soup for all to share is an example of the Zen belief that food should be divided equally between the residents of a temple, regardless of their status. This recipe uses soy sauce, but there is also a miso version. For a stronger flavor, add a little more soy sauce, miso, or saké.

serves 5–6

5 1/2 ounces (150 g) burdock root

4 dried shiitake mushrooms

2 1/2 cups (600 ml) water

1 block konnyaku, about 10 1/2 ounces (300 g), cut into bite-sized pieces

3 tablespoons sesame oil

10 1/2 ounces (300 g) daikon radish, peeled and cut into bite-sized pieces

7 ounces (200 g) carrots, peeled and cut into bite-sized pieces

3 1/2 ounces (100 g) lotus root, peeled and cut into bite-sized pieces

2 tablespoons soy sauce, for preparation

2 1/2 cups (600 ml) konbu stock (see page 98)

4 tablespoons saké

1 block firm tofu, about 14 ounces (400 g)

4 tablespoons soy sauce, for the soup

3 1/2 ounces (100 g) baby spinach or other leafy greens, cut into 2-inch (5-cm) lengths

1. Scrub the burdock root thoroughly and scrape off the skin with the back of a clean knife. Cut the burdock into bite-sized pieces, place immediately in cold water, soak for 5 minutes, then drain.

2. Soak the shiitake in the water for about 30 minutes until soft. Drain, and reserve the water. Remove the stalks, and then cut the caps into 1/4-inch (5-mm) slices.

3. Boil the konnyaku for 2 to 3 minutes, then drain.

4. Heat the sesame oil in a saucepan, then add the burdock root, shiitake, konnyaku, daikon, carrot, lotus root, and 2 tablespoons of soy sauce, and stir-fry for 5 minutes.

5. Add the shiitake water, konbu stock and saké to the saucepan, and bring to a boil over medium heat. Remove any froth from the surface, and cook on low heat until the vegetables are tender.

6. Without draining the tofu, crumble into lumps and add to the saucepan along with 4 tablespoons of soy sauce.

7. Add the baby spinach to the saucepan, and cook until wilted.

Dried shiitake

Edamame Soup

Edamame are soybeans that have been harvested when the pod is still green. Boiled in their pods with a pinch of salt, they are the perfect accompaniment to a glass of beer and are found on every bar menu in the summer. In this dish, edamame are blended into a bright green soup that tastes as refreshing as it looks.

serves 4

10 ½ ounces (300 g) fresh or frozen edamame beans, in their pods

3 ⅓ cups (800 ml) konbu stock (see page 98)

1 teaspoon salt

2 teaspoons soy sauce

4 shiso leaves, finely shredded, optional

1. Boil the edamame in their pods in salted water for 10 minutes, then drain. Shell when cool, taking care to also remove the thin inner membrane.

2. Blend the edamame and konbu stock in a food processor until smooth.

3. Pour the mixture into a saucepan, add salt and soy sauce, and simmer for 3 to 4 minutes.

4. Pour the soup into individual serving bowls, and garnish with shredded shiso leaves, if available.

Carrot and Mushroom Soymilk Soup

Delicious on its own as a healthy drink, soymilk adds a mild and mellow flavor to soups.

serves 4

3 1/2 ounces (100 g) carrot, peeled and cut into 1/2-inch (1-cm) pieces

1 2/3 cups (400 ml) soymilk

8 button mushroom or fresh shiitake mushroom caps, thinly sliced

1 2/3 cups (400 ml) konbu stock (see page 98)

2 teaspoons salt

2 tablespoons saké

carrot leaves or parsley, for garnish, optional

1. Boil the carrot in salted water for 15 minutes until soft.

2. Blend the carrot and soymilk in a food processor until smooth.

3. In a saucepan, combine the mushrooms, konbu stock, salt, and saké, and cook on medium heat for 4 to 5 minutes.

4. Add the carrot-and-soymilk mixture to the saucepan, bring to a boil, remove from the heat, and serve garnished with blanched, finely chopped carrot leaves, if available.

Turnip Rikyu Soup

The tea ceremony, still popular in Japan today, was first raised to an art form in the sixteenth century by Sen no Rikyu. Legend has it that he loved sesame, and therefore many dishes that use sesame have "Rikyu" in their names. Sesame goes well with lightly cooked, crispy turnips.

serves 4

4 small white kabu turnips, each about 2 ounces (60 g), peeled

2 tablespoons white sesame seeds

1 3/4 ounces (50 g) turnip leaves, very finely chopped

3 1/3 cups (800 ml) konbu stock (see page 98)

1 tablespoon soy sauce

1/2 teaspoon salt

2 teaspoons saké

finely grated yuzu rind, for garnish, optional

1. Cut the turnips lengthwise into 4 to 6 wedges.

2. Roast the sesame seeds (see photo), then grind in a food processor.

3. Blanch the finely chopped turnip leaves briefly in boiling salted water. Drain, and squeeze lightly.

4. In a saucepan, combine the konbu stock, soy sauce, salt, saké, and turnips, and place over medium heat for 5 to 6 minutes until the turnips are cooked through, but still crisp.

5. Add half the turnip leaves to the saucepan, bring very briefly to a boil, then remove from the heat and serve. Garnish with ground sesame, the remaining turnip leaves, and yuzu rind.

Raw sesame seeds should always be lightly roasted before using. Roast in a preheated, unoiled frying pan over low heat, shaking the pan back and forth until the seeds start to pop and release an aromatic, toasted smell.

Sesame-flavored Eggplant Soup

Eggplants fried golden brown in sesame oil are served in piping-hot konbu stock flavored with red miso. I call this dish "mirror soup" because the disks of sliced eggplant resemble small hand-mirrors.

serves 4

3 small eggplants, each about 4 ounces (120 g), sliced into ½-inch (1-cm) disks

2 tablespoons sesame oil

3⅓ cups (800 ml) konbu stock (see page 98)

2 tablespoons red miso

2 tablespoons white sesame seeds, roasted (see page 19)

1. Soak the eggplant in water for a few minutes to remove any bitterness. Drain, and dry thoroughly.

2. Heat a frying pan, add the sesame oil, then add the eggplant. Cook both sides over medium heat for 5 to 6 minutes.

3. In a saucepan, heat the konbu stock, then stir in the red miso until dissolved.

4. Divide the eggplant slices between individual soup bowls, and cover with the stock.

5. Crush the roasted white sesame seeds, and sprinkle them over the soup.

SALADS

Shojin Salad with Peanut-flavored Tofu Dressing

This creamy peanut, lemon, and tofu dressing is a great way to enhance the taste of fresh vegetables.

serves 4

8 thin spears asparagus, with woody ends removed

4 lettuce leaves, torn into bite-sized pieces

10 ½ ounces (300 g) tomatoes, cut in ½-inch (1-cm) dice

2 avocados, cut in ½-inch (1-cm) dice

2 Japanese cucumbers, cut in ½-inch (1-cm) dice

dressing

1 block tofu (silken, if available), about 7 ounces (200 g)

2 tablespoons peanut butter, unsweetened type

2 tablespoons rice vinegar or any white vinegar

2 tablespoons olive oil

2 teaspoons maple syrup

dash black pepper

1 teaspoon salt

2 tablespoons lemon juice

1. Wrap the tofu in a paper towel or tea towel (see photo), place a plate on top and refrigerate for about 30 minutes to remove excess moisture.

2. To make the dressing, blend the tofu, peanut butter, rice vinegar, olive oil, maple syrup, black pepper, salt, and lemon juice in a food processor.

3. Blanch the asparagus in boiling water, drain, plunge into cold water, then slice diagonally into 1-inch (2–3-cm) pieces.

4. Spread the lettuce on a serving plate, arrange the asparagus, tomato, avocado and cucumber on top, and cover with the dressing.

Wrap the tofu in a tea towel to remove excess moisture.

Soybean and Sukikonbu Salad with Lemon-Miso Dressing

Dried seaweed, such as konbu or wakame, is widely used in Japanese cuisine and is surprisingly easy to cook with. This recipe uses sukikonbu, a type of seaweed dried into easy-to-cut flat sheets. If sukikonbu is not available, use regular dried konbu.

serves 4

1 sheet sukikonbu, about 5 1/2 x 4 inches (14 x 10 cm) square, or 1 piece dried konbu about 4 inches (10 cm) square.

1/3 cup (5 g) dried wakame seaweed

1/2 cup (85 g) cooked soybeans

1 sprig sansho, for garnish, optional

dressing

3 tablespoons lemon juice

2 tablespoons white miso, or 1 tablespoon red miso

2 tablespoons rice vinegar or any white vinegar

2 teaspoons maple syrup

2 teaspoons olive oil

2 tablespoons finely chopped parsley

1. Shred the sukikonbu into thin 1 1/2-inch (3–4-cm) lengths, soak in cold water for 10 minutes (see photo), then drain in a colander. Place in a saucepan of water, bring to a boil, then reduce the heat to medium and cook for 10 minutes.

2. Soak the wakame in cold water for 10 minutes, then drain. Blanch briefly in boiling water then cut into bite-sized pieces.

3. To make the dressing, combine the lemon juice, miso, rice vinegar, maple syrup, olive oil, and parsley, and mix well.

4. Add the seaweed and soybeans to the bowl of dressing, mix well until the ingredients are coated, then serve garnished with a sprig of sansho.

Soak the sukikonbu in cold water.

Carrot, Cucumber and Celery Salad with a Miso Dip

Miso, a fermented soybean paste, is one of Japan's most traditional seasonings. Found in white, red and almost-black varieties, it is most commonly used in miso soup, but can also add a rich flavor to dips and dressings.

serves 4

7 ounces (200 g) carrots, peeled and sliced into thin 4-inch (10-cm) lengths

2 Japanese cucumbers, sliced into thin 4-inch (10-cm) lengths

2 celery stalks, with strings removed, and sliced into thin 4-inch (10-cm) lengths

dip

2 tablespoons red miso

2 tablespoons maple syrup

2 tablespoons lemon juice

2 tablespoons sesame oil

2 tablespoons red wine

2 tablespoons rice vinegar or any white vinegar

2 teaspoons finely chopped peanuts

1. To make the dip, combine the red miso, maple syrup, lemon juice, sesame oil, red wine, rice vinegar, and peanuts.
2. Pour the dip into a deep bowl, and stand the vegetable sticks in it.

Broccoli and Cauliflower Salad with Tofu Dressing

Broccoli and cauliflower are from the same vegetable family and both are rich in vitamin C. In this recipe, they are cooked al dente, and served with a sesame-flavored tofu dressing.

serves 4

7 ounces (200 g) broccoli, separated into small florets

7 ounces (200 g) cauliflower, separated into small florets

dressing

1 block firm tofu, about 3 ½ ounces (100 g)

1 tablespoon white miso, or 1 teaspoon red miso

1 tablespoon white sesame seeds, roasted and ground (see page 19)

3 tablespoons rice vinegar or any white vinegar

2 tablespoons olive oil

1 tablespoon white wine

1. Wrap the tofu in a paper towel or tea towel (see page 24), place a plate on top and refrigerate for about 30 minutes to remove excess moisture.

2. Boil the broccoli and cauliflower in salted water for 5 to 6 minutes, occasionally testing the florets with a fork to make sure they do not overcook.

3. To make the dressing, blend the tofu, miso, sesame, rice vinegar, olive oil, and white wine in a food processor.

4. Arrange the vegetables on a serving plate, and top with the tofu dressing.

Eggplant Salad with Lemon-flavored Plum Dressing

Eggplants are so delicious in the fall that it is easy to overindulge. Eating too many can have a cooling effect on the body, which is thought to be particularly bad for women. Perhaps this is the origin of the old Japanese saying "Don't let your daughter-in-law eat autumn eggplants."

serves 4

4 small eggplants, each about
   3 1/2 ounces (100 g)

3 or 4 shiso leaves, finely shredded,
   optional

dressing

2 tablespoons pickled plum paste

3 tablespoons lemon juice

2 teaspoons maple syrup

2 tablespoons olive oil

1 teaspoon salt

1. Slice the eggplant lengthwise, then cut into bite-sized pieces and soak in water for about 5 minutes. Drain, and squeeze to remove excess liquid.

2. To make the dressing, combine the pickled plum paste, lemon juice, maple syrup, olive oil, and salt, and mix well.

3. Bring a pan of water to a boil, add the eggplant, and cook for 3 to 4 minutes. Alternatively, fry the eggplant in 2 tablespoons of olive oil.

4. Arrange the eggplant on a serving plate, and drizzle with the dressing. Garnish with shredded shiso, if available.

Shiso leaves

Spinach and Arugula Salad with Piquant Dressing

Usu-age tofu is sold in ready-made deep-fried slices. Roasted usu-age pieces and almonds add a crunchy texture to this spicy, colorful dish.

serves 4

7 ounces (200 g) salad spinach

4 ounces (120 g) arugula

2 slices usu-age tofu, cut into small pieces

1 tablespoon sliced almonds

4 cherry tomatoes, halved or quartered

4 or 5 grapefruit segments, roughly chopped

dressing

4 tablespoons olive oil

2 tablespoons lemon juice

2 tablespoons rice vinegar or any white vinegar

1/2 teaspoon shichimi pepper or chili powder

dash black pepper

1/2 teaspoon salt

2 teaspoons maple syrup

2 teaspoons soy sauce

1. Wash the spinach and arugula, plunge into iced water to crisp, tear the leaves into bite-sized pieces, then pat dry.

2. Roast the usu-age with the almonds in a preheated, unoiled frying pan for 1 to 2 minutes.

3. To make the dressing, combine the olive oil, lemon juice, rice vinegar, shichimi pepper, black pepper, salt, maple syrup, and soy sauce, and mix well.

4. Arrange the lettuce and arugula on a serving plate, and place the tomatoes, grapefruit, usu-age, and almonds on top. Drizzle with the dressing.

Lentil, Cucumber and Mushroom Salad

Lentils are easy to cook. Just boil them up and they're done. An Indian friend living in my neighborhood taught me this recipe, but the dressing is my own.

serves 4

½ cup (85 g) dried green lentils

½ cup (85 g) dried red lentils

2 tablespoons olive oil

8 button mushroom caps, thinly sliced

2 Japanese cucumbers, thinly sliced on the diagonal

2 tablespoons lemon juice

dressing

2 tablespoons olive oil

2 tablespoons lemon juice

1 teaspoon salt

1 teaspoon curry powder

2 teaspoons soy sauce

2 tablespoons white wine

2 tablespoons rice vinegar or any white vinegar

1. Boil the green and red lentils together in the same saucepan for 10 to 15 minutes until soft, then drain, place in a bowl and mix in the olive oil.

2. Blanch the mushrooms in hot water, and drain. Place the cucumber and mushrooms in a bowl, and mix with 2 tablespoons of lemon juice.

3. To make the dressing, combine the olive oil, 2 tablespoons of lemon juice, salt, curry powder, soy sauce, white wine, and rice vinegar, and mix well.

4. Add the lentils, cucumber slices and mushrooms to the dressing, mix well, and serve.

Cannellini Bean and Wakame Salad with Lemon Dressing

Peas, edamame beans, soybeans or any mixture of variously colored beans can be substituted for the cannellini beans. Wakame seaweed and beans are both high in fiber, making this salad both nutritious and tasty.

serves 4

1 cup (170 g) cooked red kidney beans, drained

1 cup (170 g) cooked cannellini beans, drained

2 tablespoons lemon juice

⅓ cup (5 g) dried wakame seaweed

dressing

4 tablespoons lemon juice

4 tablespoons grapeseed oil

2 tablespoons rice vinegar or any white vinegar

dash black pepper

1 teaspoon salt

2 tablespoons white wine

1. Mix the kidney beans and cannellini beans, then sprinkle with 2 table-spoons of lemon juice.

2. Soak the wakame in cold water for 10 minutes to reconstitute, blanch briefly in boiling water, drain, and cut into bite-sized pieces.

3. To make the dressing, combine the 4 tablespoons of lemon juice, grape-seed oil, rice vinegar, black pepper, salt, and white wine, and mix well.

4. Add the beans and wakame to the dressing, and mix well.

Sweet Potato and Soybeans with Miso and Lemon Sauce

Mashed potato is the base for this original sauce.

serves 4

10 ounces (300 g) sweet potato, unpeeled and cut in $1/2$-inch (1-cm) dice

$1/2$ cup (85 g) cooked soybeans

1 tablespoon lemon juice

2–3 lettuce leaves

2–3 arugula leaves

sauce

2 ounces (60 g) potato, peeled and cut into bite-sized pieces

1 tablespoon white miso, or 1 teaspoon red miso

1 tablespoon sesame oil

1 tablespoon lemon juice

1 tablespoon rice vinegar or any white vinegar

1 teaspoon maple syrup

2 tablespoons white wine

$1/2$ teaspoon salt

Sweet potatoes

1. Cook the sweet potato in salted water on medium heat until soft. Drain, place in a bowl, and toss with the soybeans and lemon juice.

2. Place the potato in a saucepan with just enough salted water to cover, and bring to the boil. Lower the heat to medium and cook for 10 minutes. When cooked through, drain any excess liquid, then mash until smooth.

3. To make the sauce, blend the mashed potato, miso, sesame oil, lemon juice, rice vinegar, maple syrup, white wine, and salt in a food processor.

4. Arrange the lettuce and arugula leaves on a serving plate and top with the sweet potato and soybean mixture, and the dressing.

TOFU and BEANS

Tofu with Mushroom Sauce

Nutritious tofu is served with a sauce of fall mushrooms, a dish to warm the body as the days grow cooler.

1 block tofu, silken if available, about 14 ounces (400 g)

1³/4 ounces (50 g) mushroom caps, 2 or 3 types, for example, shimeji, enoki, fresh shiitake, or button

1²/3 cups (400 ml) konbu stock (see page 98)

2 tablespoons soy sauce

2 tablespoons saké

2 tablespoons mirin

1 tablespoon sugar

1 teaspoon salt

1¹/4 ounces (40 g) carrot, peeled and julienned

2 tablespoons cornstarch, dissolved in 4 tablespoons water

Strips of green beans, blanched, for garnish, optional

1. Wrap the tofu in a paper towel or tea towel (see page 24), place a plate on top and refrigerate for 30 minutes to remove excess moisture.

2. Break the shimeji and enoki into bite-sized pieces, and cut the other mushrooms into thin slices.

3. In a frying pan, combine the konbu stock, soy sauce, saké, mirin, sugar, and salt, bring to a boil, then add the mushrooms and carrot. Lower the heat to medium and cook for a further 3 to 4 minutes.

4. Cut the tofu in half and place in the frying pan, taking care that the tofu halves do not overlap. Cook on low heat for 5 minutes.

5. Add the dissolved cornstarch to the frying pan, and stir gently, without breaking the tofu, until the sauce thickens.

6. Cut the tofu into 4 pieces and serve hot in individual bowls, topped with the mushroom sauce, and garnished with a green bean strip.

Tofu Fried with Almonds

Tofu is a light and simple ingredient that can be cooked in many ways for a variety of flavors. Deep-fried tofu is particularly delicious. In this dish, the tofu is encrusted with almond slices before frying. The outside is crispy and aromatic, while the inside is soft and moist. This dish tastes best served hot with a sprinkling of lemon juice.

2 blocks firm tofu, about 1³/₄ pounds (800 g) in total

1 teaspoon salt

dash white pepper

³/₈ cup (45 g) all-purpose flour

¹/₅ cup (50 ml) water

⁵/₈ cup (50 g) sliced almonds

vegetable oil, for deep-frying

salt, for serving

¹/₂ lemon, cut into wedges

Coat the tofu pieces with almond slices.

1. Wrap the tofu in a paper towel or tea towel (see page 24), cover with a plate and refrigerate for 30 minutes to remove excess moisture.

2. Cut each block of tofu into 6 pieces, and sprinkle with salt and pepper.

3. To make the batter, mix the flour and water. The batter should be slightly lumpy. Coat the tofu pieces first with batter, then with almond slices (see photo).

4. Heat the vegetable oil to 360°F (180°C), add the tofu pieces, and deep-fry until golden brown.

5. Arrange on a serving plate with salt or lemon wedges.

Natto and Okra with Yuzu

Natto, made from fermented soybeans, has a pungent aroma and sticky consistency. A taste well worth acquiring, natto is both versatile and healthy, served here with vitamin-rich okra and a tangy yuzu dressing.

serves 4

6 okra

2 packs natto, about 3 1/2 ounces (100 g) in total

finely grated yuzu rind, for garnish

dressing

1 1/2 teaspoons yuzu juice

1 1/2 teaspoons soy sauce

1. To make the dressing, mix the yuzu juice and soy sauce in a small bowl.

2. Boil the okra for 1 to 2 minutes, or until just tender, then immediately plunge into cold water. Drain, and thinly slice.

3. Place the natto and okra in a bowl, and mix well until sticky. Add the yuzu dressing and mix again.

4. Transfer to individual serving dishes and garnish with yuzu rind.

Pea and Cauliflower Stew

Fresh green and white colors add a taste of spring to this dish.

⁴/₅ cup (200 ml) konbu stock (see page 98)

3½ ounces (100 g) shelled peas

7 ounces (200 g) cauliflower, separated into bite-sized florets

1 teaspoon salt

2 tablespoons saké or white wine

1½ tablespoons white miso

⁴/₅ cup (200 ml) soymilk

1. In a saucepan, bring the konbu stock to a boil. Lower the heat to medium, add the peas, cauliflower, salt, and saké, and cook for 10 minutes.

2. Dissolve the miso into the stock, then add the soymilk. Bring to a boil, then turn off the heat.

3. Ladle the stew into serving bowls.

*Do not let this dish simmer after the soymilk has been added. The soymilk's flavor peaks the moment it is heated.

Deep-Fried Yuba Rolls

Yuba is the skin that forms on the surface of boiled soymilk. Sold dried into sheets, it is a high-protein ingredient with a variety of uses.

makes 8

8 slices dried yuba, each about 8 inches (20 cm) square

2 ounces (60 g) nagaimo yam, peeled and finely diced

8 fresh shiitake or button mushroom caps, finely diced

½ ounce (15 g) carrot, peeled and finely chopped

1 teaspoon salt

dash white pepper

2 tablespoons cornstarch

2 tablespoons all-purpose flour, dissolved in 2 tablespoons water

vegetable oil, for deep-frying

salt, for garnish

1. Wrap each slice of dried yuba in a wet cloth, and leave for about 30 minutes until soft.

2. Place the yam, shiitake, and carrot in a bowl, sprinkle with salt, pepper, and cornstarch, and mix well.

3. Lay out the yuba slices, divide the vegetables into 8 equal portions and place each portion on top of a yuba slice. Fold the yuba over to make rectangular envelopes, and seal using the flour-and-water mixture. Preheat the oil to 340°F (170°C) and deep-fry the envelopes until golden brown.

4. Cut the yuba envelopes in half and arrange on a serving dish, garnished with salt.

*If yuba is not available, use rice-paper wrappers.

Yuba

Koyadofu Teriyaki

A monk on Mount Koya once left some tofu outside overnight in winter. Next morning, the tofu was frozen, but he cooked it anyway and was surprised to find it delicious. Ever since, frozen tofu has been known as koyadofu and is a widely used ingredient. In this dish, reconstituted koyadofu is soaked in a konbu-flavored broth and then pan-fried, teriyaki style, in sesame oil. The rich sesame aroma is truly mouthwatering.

serves 4

4 cakes koyadofu, about 3 ounces (80 g) in total

1 cup (240 ml) konbu stock (see page 98)

2 tablespoons sugar

3 tablespoons soy sauce

2 tablespoons sesame oil or olive oil

finely grated yuzu rind, for garnish

Soak the koyadofu in hot water to reconstitute.

1. Soak the koyadofu in hot water for 2 to 3 minutes to reconstitute (see photo), then remove and squeeze gently to remove excess moisture.

2. In a saucepan combine the konbu stock, sugar, and soy sauce, bring to a boil, then add the koyadofu, and cook for a further 5 to 6 minutes on low. Turn off the heat and let sit for 7 to 8 minutes. Remove the koyadofu from the broth and gently squeeze out the liquid.

3. Heat the sesame oil in a frying pan, add the koyadofu and fry on low to medium heat for 1 to 2 minutes on each side, until golden brown.

4. Arrange the koyadofu on a serving plate and garnish with yuzu rind.

*4 tablespoons of commercially available teriyaki sauce can be substituted for the sugar and soy sauce.

Natto and Potato Salad

7 ounces (200 g) potato, peeled and cut
in ½-inch (1-cm) dice

2 packs natto, about 3 ½ ounces (100 g)
in total

½ teaspoon karashi mustard

1 ½ teaspoons soy sauce

6–8 shiso leaves, finely shredded

1. Soak the potato in cold water for a minute, boil in salted water for about
   10 minutes until tender, then drain.

2. In a bowl, stir the natto until sticky, add the karashi mustard and soy
   sauce, and mix again.

3. When the potato is cool, gently toss with the natto mixture, and garnish
   with shredded shiso.

Soybeans in Vegetable-Miso Sauce

serves 2 or 3

1 ¾ ounces (50 g) burdock root

2 dried shiitake mushrooms

⅔ ounce (20 g) green beans, thinly sliced

2 tablespoons red miso

2 tablespoons sugar

2 tablespoons saké

½ teaspoon finely minced fresh ginger

2 tablespoons sesame oil

1 ¾ ounces (50 g) carrot, peeled and
cut in ½-inch (1-cm) dice

⅓ cup (50 g) cooked soybeans

dash shichimi pepper, optional

1. Clean and scrape the burdock root (see page 99), cut into ½-inch
   (1-cm) pieces, and soak in cold water for 5 minutes.

2. Soak the shiitake in water for 30 minutes to reconstitute,
   remove the hard tips from the stems, then dice.

3. Boil the green beans in salted water for 2 to 3 minutes.

4. In a bowl, combine the red miso with the sugar and
   1 tablespoon of the saké, and mix well.

5. Fry the ginger in the sesame oil for 2 minutes, then
   add the burdock root, shiitake and carrot, and fry
   until cooked through. Mix in the soybeans and the
   remaining 1 tablespoon of saké.

6. Add the miso to the pan and stir over low heat for 5 minutes. Then add the green beans and continue stirring for
   2 to 3 minutes.

7. Divide the mixture between individual serving bowls, and sprinkle
   with shichimi pepper.

Miso-Pickled Tofu

Buddhist monks are expected to avoid alcohol, but you will find that this strongly flavored side dish goes very well with saké!

serves 4

1 block firm tofu, about 14 ounces (400 g)

2 ounces (60 g) red miso

3 tablespoons saké

1 tablespoon sugar

1 sprig sansho, for garnish, optional

1. Wrap the tofu in a paper towel or tea towel (see page 24), place a plate on top and refrigerate for 30 minutes to remove excess moisture.

2. In a bowl, combine the red miso, saké, and sugar, and mix well.

3. Lay out a sheet of gauze (or plastic wrap) large enough to wrap the tofu in, and thinly spread the miso mixture over it. Place the tofu on top of the miso, and wrap it in the gauze.

4. Refrigerate overnight (in a sealed container if the tofu is gauze-wrapped). Remove the tofu from the wrap and wipe off the miso with a paper towel. Thinly slice the tofu and arrange on a serving plate, garnished with sansho.

Steamed Pumpkin and Tofu

The simple, light flavor of Japanese pumpkin lends itself well to a variety of cooking methods. In this recipe pumpkin is steamed to bring out its sweetness without losing its firm texture.

serves 4

1 block firm tofu, about 7 ounces (200 g)

1 small kikuza or kurokawa pumpkin, about 1 pound 5 ounces (600 g)

small can mixed vegetables, about 3 1/2 ounces (100 g), drained

1 tablespoon cornstarch

dash salt

sauce

1 2/3 cups (400 ml) konbu stock (see page 98)

3 tablespoons sugar

3 tablespoons soy sauce

3 tablespoons cornstarch dissolved in 3 tablespoons water

1. Wrap the tofu in a paper towel or tea towel (see page 24), place a plate on top and leave for 30 minutes to remove excess moisture.

2. Cut the pumpkin in half vertically and scoop out the seeds and stringy fibers.

3. In a bowl, mix the tofu, mixed vegetables, 1 tablespoon of cornstarch, and salt into a smooth, firm paste. Stuff the mixture into the scooped out hollow of each pumpkin half.

4. Steam the stuffed pumpkin in a preheated steamer for 20 to 30 minutes until the flesh is tender.

5. To make the sauce, combine the konbu stock, sugar, and soy sauce in a saucepan, and mix well. Bring to a boil over medium heat, then add the cornstarch-and-water mixture. Stir until the sauce thickens.

6. Cut the pumpkin into wedges, arrange on a serving plate, and top with the sauce.

VEGETABLES

Asparagus and Hijiki with White Vinegar Dressing

serves 4

½ cup (20 g) dried hijiki seaweed

12 thin spears asparagus, with woody ends removed

2 teaspoons soy sauce

dressing

1 block firm tofu, about 3½ ounces (100 g)

2 tablespoons white sesame seeds, roasted and ground (see page 19)

2 teaspoons white miso, or 1 teaspoon red miso

3 tablespoons rice vinegar or lemon juice

1 tablespoon sugar

½ teaspoon salt

1. Wrap the tofu in a paper towel or tea towel (see page 24), place a plate on top and refrigerate for 30 minutes to remove excess moisture.

2. Soak the dried hijiki in water for about 15 minutes to reconstitute, boil for about 1 minute until soft, then drain.

3. Blanch the asparagus in boiling salted water, drain, then plunge briefly into cold water. Cut into 1½-inch (3–4-cm) lengths, place in a bowl, then sprinkle with the soy sauce while still hot.

4. To make the dressing, combine the tofu, sesame, miso, rice vinegar, sugar, and salt, and mix to a smooth paste.

5. Arrange the hijiki and asparagus on a serving plate and top with the dressing.

Fried Pumpkin with Peanut Sauce

serves 4

4 tablespoons sesame oil or olive oil

14 ounces (400 g) kikuza or kurokawa pumpkin, with seeds and stringy fibers removed, and sliced into very thin wedges

sauce

6 tablespoons peanut butter, unsweet-ened type

2 teaspoons white miso, or 1 teaspoon red miso

2 tablespoons saké or white wine

3 tablespoons lemon juice

2 tablespoons mirin, or 1 tablespoon sugar

1. Heat the sesame oil in a frying pan, add the pumpkin and fry, covered, over medium heat for 10 to 15 minutes, turning occasionally until both sides start to change color. Alternatively, baste the pumpkin with sesame oil, and roast in the oven at 320°F (160°C) for 15 minutes.

2. To make the sauce, combine the peanut butter, miso, saké, lemon juice, and mirin, and mix well.

3. Arrange the pumpkin on a serving plate, and top with the peanut sauce.

Asparagus and Carrots with Walnut Dressing

serves 4

10 thin spears asparagus, with woody ends removed

4 ounces (120 g) carrots, peeled and finely sliced into 1-inch (2–3-cm) matchsticks

2 tablespoons lemon juice

dressing

2 ounces (60 g) walnuts

2 teaspoons white miso, or 1 teaspoon red miso

2 tablespoons mirin

2 teaspoons soy sauce

2 tablespoons olive oil

2 tablespoons white wine

2 tablespoons rice vinegar or any white vinegar

1. Cook the asparagus for about 2 minutes in a saucepan of boiling, salted water, taking care not to overcook, then cut into 1-inch (2–3-cm) lengths on the diagonal. Boil the carrots for 2 minutes, then drain. Sprinkle the vegetables with lemon juice while still hot.

2. To make the dressing, blend together the walnuts, miso, mirin, soy sauce, olive oil, white wine, and rice vinegar, using a food processor.

3. Mix the carrots and asparagus with the dressing, and arrange on a serving plate.

Mushrooms and Spinach with Yuzu Dressing

serves 4

4 large fresh shiitake mushroom caps,
   each about 3 inches (8 cm) in diameter

2 tablespoons freshly squeezed yuzu juice

7 ounces (200 g) spinach

soy sauce, about 2 tablespoons

1 teaspoon sugar

2 teaspoons grated yuzu rind

1. Grill the shiitake on low heat, turning until both sides have changed color. Thinly slice, then sprinkle with 1 tablespoon of the yuzu juice.

2. Blanch the spinach in hot water, plunge briefly into cold water to remove any bitterness, squeeze, and cut into 1-inch (2–3-cm) lengths. Sprinkle with 2 teaspoons of the soy sauce and squeeze again to remove excess water and also to allow the soy sauce flavor to soak into the spinach.

3. In a bowl, combine the remaining 1 tablespoon of yuzu juice, the remaining soy sauce, and the sugar, and mix well. Add the shiitake and spinach, and toss gently.

4. Arrange the vegetables on a serving plate and garnish with grated yuzu rind.

Steamed Mushrooms with Yam Sauce

In Japan, yam is often grated and blanched, dressed with vinegar and served as a salad. In this recipe, nagaimo yam is blended into a smooth sauce and steamed with simmered mushrooms. The yam's mellow taste harmonizes delightfully with the juicy mushrooms.

serves 4

4 dried shiitake mushrooms

1 ¼ cups (300 ml) water

2 ounces (60 g) shimeji mushrooms, separated into 2 or 3 clusters

2 ounces (60 g) enoki mushrooms, cut into 2 clusters

4 fresh shiitake mushrooms, thinly sliced

8 button mushrooms, thinly sliced

1 tablespoon soy sauce

1 tablespoon saké

½ teaspoon salt

8 ½ ounces (240 g) nagaimo yam, peeled and roughly chopped

2 teaspoons lemon or lime juice

finely grated lemon or lime rind, for garnish, optional

soy sauce, to taste

1. Soak the dried shiitake in the water for about 30 minutes, remove the stems, and thinly slice the caps. Reserve the shiitake water.

2. Place the shiitake water, mushrooms, soy sauce, saké, and salt in a saucepan. Bring to a boil, then simmer for 5 to 6 minutes on medium heat. Occasionally remove any froth from the surface.

3. Blend the yam in a food processor until smooth.

4. Divide the mushrooms and the cooking sauce between individual heat-proof serving dishes, top each dish with the yam, and cook in a preheated steamer for 4 to 5 minutes on medium heat. If a steamer is not available, cover with aluminum foil and cook in the oven over a tray of water at 360°F (180°C) for 6 to 7 minutes.

5. Serve immediately, sprinkled with lemon juice and garnished with rind. Add a few drops of soy sauce to taste.

Eringi Mushrooms with Vegetable-Miso Dressing

Eringi mushrooms fried in sesame oil have a lovely crunchy texture.

serves 4

7 ounces (200 g) eringi mushrooms, cut into thin vertical slices

4 tablespoons sesame oil

2–3 tablespoons lemon juice

1/4 teaspoon salt

4 fresh shiitake mushrooms caps, finely chopped

1 ounce (30 g) green beans, with strings removed, and cut into 1/8-inch (2–3-mm) pieces

1/2 ounce (15 g) carrot, peeled and finely chopped

3 tablespoons grapeseed oil or vegetable oil

2 tablespoons red miso

4 tablespoons saké or white wine

2 tablespoons sugar

2 tablespoons crushed walnuts

1. Fry the eringi in the sesame oil for 10 minutes, turning occasionally. Arrange on a serving plate and sprinkle with lemon juice and salt.

2. For the dressing, sauté the shiitake, green beans and carrot in the grapeseed oil over medium heat for 2 to 3 minutes. Turn the heat to low, and add the red miso, saké, and sugar, and stir for a further 2 to 3 minutes.

3. Cover the eringi with the dressing and garnish with walnuts.

Shiitake Mushrooms Stuffed with Tofu

In temple cuisine, vegetable ingredients are sometimes used to imitate shellfish or seafood. This fun dish uses shiitake mushrooms and tofu to imitate the shape of the shellfish abalone.

makes 8

1 block tofu, silken if available, about 10 1/2 ounces (300 g)

2 tablespoons mirin

2 tablespoons soy sauce

2 tablespoons white sesame seeds, roasted (see page 19)

1/2 teaspoon salt

8 large fresh shiitake mushroom caps, each about 3 inches (8 cm) in diameter

all-purpose flour, for dusting

sesame oil, for frying

4 shiso leaves, finely shredded, optional

Evenly dust the undersides of the mushroom caps with flour until the radial lines disappear.

1. Wrap the tofu in a paper towel or tea towel (see page 24), place a plate on top and refrigerate for 30 minutes to remove excess moisture.

2. In a saucepan, mix the mirin and soy sauce, boil for 1 to 2 minutes, then set aside.

3. Grind the sesame seeds, then blend with the tofu and salt, using a food processor.

4. Evenly dust the undersides of the shiitake caps with flour (see photo).

5. Fill the shiitake caps with a generous quantity of the tofu mixture, then fry both sides in sesame oil over medium heat for 5 to 6 minutes. Add the mirin-and-soy sauce mixture to the pan, turn the heat to low, and cook, shaking the pan occasionally, until the liquid evaporates.

6. Arrange the shiitake on a serving plate, garnished with the shredded shiso leaves.

*4 tablespoons of commercially available teriyaki sauce can be substituted for the mirin and soy sauce.

Mashed Taro

Taro, a kind of potato in season through fall and winter, is delicious mashed and mixed with other vegetables. When peeled, taro becomes sticky, so make sure to rub salt on the outside before cooking.

serves 4

4 dried shiitake mushrooms	2 tablespoons soy sauce
8 taro, each about 1 3/4 ounces (50 g), peeled and cut into 1/2-inch (1-cm) rounds	1 ounce (30 g) carrot, peeled and finely chopped
1 teaspoon salt	2/3 ounce (20 g) green beans, finely chopped
2 1/2 cups (600 ml) konbu stock (see page 98)	2 tablespoons cornstarch, dissolved in 4 tablespoons water
2 tablespoons sugar	a little grated ginger, for garnish

1. Soak the shiitake in water for about 30 minutes to reconstitute, remove the stalks, then chop the caps very finely.

2. Rub the taro with the salt, then rinse.

3. In a saucepan, combine the konbu stock, sugar and soy sauce, and place over medium heat. When the sugar has dissolved, add the taro and cook for about 20 minutes until soft. Remove the taro, and reserve the stock.

4. Add the shiitake, carrot and green beans to the taro stock, and cook for 5 to 6 minutes over medium heat. Drain thoroughly, and reserve the stock.

5. Mash the taro while still hot (see photo). Divide into 8 portions and place each portion on top of a sheet of plastic wrap. Place a spoonful of the vegetable mixture on top of each portion. Lift each corner of the plastic wrap and close over the top of each portion, forming a ball. The vegetable mixture should be partly inside the ball, and partly visible at the top of the ball.

6. Remove the plastic wrap and arrange the balls on a serving plate.

7. In a saucepan, combine 1 cup (240 ml) of taro stock with the dissolved cornstarch mixture and stir over low heat until thick. Pour the thickened sauce over the taro balls and garnish with grated ginger.

Mash the taro while still hot.

Avocado Sashimi

In this recipe, mashed avocado is set in agar-agar for a sashimi-like texture.

1 avocado, about 6 ounces (170 g)

3 teaspoons agar-agar powder

⁴/₅ cup (200 ml) konbu stock (see page 98)

¹/₄ teaspoon salt

¹/₂ teaspoon wasabi paste

1 tablespoon soy sauce

lemon wedges, optional

1. Scrape out the flesh of the avocado, and blend in a food processor with the agar-agar powder, konbu stock, and salt, until smooth.

2. Place the avocado mixture in a saucepan, bring to a boil over medium heat, and then pour into 4 individual serving dishes. When the mixture has cooled to room temperature, refrigerate for 30 to 40 minutes.

3. Serve with wasabi mixed with soy sauce, or with a squeeze of lemon juice.

*The jelly can also be set in a large dish and then cut into individual portions.

Asparagus and Carrot Soymilk Jelly

This colorful and attractive cold dish is ideal for parties.

serves 4

1³/₄ ounces (50 g) carrot, peeled and finely diced

3 or 4 thin spears asparagus, with woody ends removed, and cut into ¹/₂-inch (1-cm) pieces

⁴/₅ cup (200 ml) konbu stock (see page 98)

3 teaspoons agar-agar powder

⁴/₅ cup (200 ml) soymilk

sauce

²/₅ cup (100 ml) konbu stock (see page 98)

2 teaspoons soy sauce

2 teaspoons sugar

2 teaspoons cornstarch dissolved in 2 teaspoons water

1. To make the sauce, place the ²/₅ cup (100 ml) of konbu stock, the soy sauce, and sugar in a saucepan, and bring to a boil. Lower the heat to medium, stir in the water-and-cornstarch mixture until the sauce thickens, then remove from the heat and refrigerate.

2. Boil the carrot for 5 minutes in salted water, then add the asparagus to the pan and boil for a further 1 minute. Remove from the heat, and drain well.

3. Place the ⁴/₅ cup (200 ml) of konbu stock and the agar-agar in a saucepan, and bring to a boil, stirring constantly. Turn the heat to low, add the soymilk, and cook for a further 5 minutes, continuing to stir.

4. Pour the soymilk mixture into individual serving dishes, then add equal amounts of carrot and asparagus to each dish. When the mixture has cooled to room temperature, refrigerate for at least an hour until set, then serve topped with the sauce.

Eggplant with Edamame Dressing

In this dish, eggplants are dressed with an edamame paste, a mouth-watering bright green. For a smooth paste, cook the edamame until they are completely soft.

serves 4

4 eggplants, each about 3 ½ ounces (100 g)

4 tablespoons sesame oil

1 tablespoon sugar

2 tablespoons soy sauce

sprigs of sansho, for garnish, optional

dressing

8 ½ ounces (240 g) edamame beans, in their pods

⅖ cup (100 ml) konbu stock (see page 98)

2 teaspoons rice vinegar or any white vinegar

2 tablespoons mirin

¼ teaspoon salt

1. To make the dressing, boil the edamame beans for 20 minutes, then shell, taking care to also remove the thin inner membrane. Place the beans in a food processor, gradually add the konbu stock, and blend to a smooth paste. Turn off the food processor, then add the vinegar, mirin, and salt.

2. Cut the eggplants in half, and then cut into long strips about ⅛ inch (3–5 mm) wide. Fry in the sesame oil, stirring gently. When soft, stir in the sugar and soy sauce to coat, then remove from the heat.

3. Arrange the eggplants on a serving plate and top with the edamame dressing. Garnish with sansho.

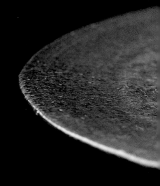

Sweet Potato with Green Vinegar Dressing

Deep-fried sweet potato is seasoned with a cucumber and vinegar dressing. The gold of the fried potato contrasts with the green of the cucumber to make a colorful and appetizing dish.

serves 4

vegetable oil, for deep-frying

10 ½ ounces (300 g) sweet potato, unpeeled, and diced into ½-inch (1-cm) pieces

dressing

2 Japanese cucumbers

3 tablespoons rice vinegar or any white vinegar

1 tablespoon sugar

1. Heat the vegetable oil to 340°F (170°C) and deep-fry the sweet potato for about 10 minutes.

2. Put the cucumbers unpeeled into a food processor, blend to a rough paste, then wrap in a paper towel to absorb any excess liquid.

3. To make the dressing, combine the cucumber, rice vinegar, and sugar, and mix well.

4. Arrange the sweet potato on a serving plate and drizzle with the cucumber dressing.

Carrot Croquettes

Croquettes are very popular with children in Japan, and are usually made by mixing ground meat with mashed potato, coating in breadcrumbs, and deep-frying. This recipe uses carrots and tofu instead of meat and potato, to make surprisingly light croquettes. The key to making this dish is the removal of all excess moisture from the tofu.

makes 14

1 block firm tofu, about 1 pound (450 g)

10 ½ ounces (300 g) carrots, peeled, and sliced into thin half-rounds

1 teaspoon salt

2 tablespoons roughly chopped walnuts or crushed peanuts

2 tablespoons cornstarch

all purpose flour, for dusting

⅓ cup (40 g) all-purpose flour, mixed with 3 tablespoons water

1 cup (60 g) dried breadcrumbs

vegetable oil, for deep-frying

1 lemon or lime, cut into wedges

1. Wrap the tofu in a paper towel or tea towel (see page 24), place a plate on top and refrigerate for 30 minutes to remove excess moisture.

2. Boil the carrots for 10 minutes in just enough water to cover until soft, then drain. Return the carrots to the pan and place over low heat until any remaining liquid evaporates, then mash.

3. In a bowl, combine the tofu, mashed carrots, salt, walnuts, and cornstarch, and mix well. Divide the mixture into 14 oval-shaped croquettes and dust evenly with flour.

4. Coat the croquettes with the flour-and-water mixture, dip in the bread-crumbs and deep-fry for 2 to 3 minutes in vegetable oil preheated to 340–360°F (170–180°C), until golden brown.

5. Arrange on a serving plate and garnish with lemon wedges.

*Carrot croquettes are also delicious pan-fried in olive oil. The croquettes should be flattened slightly so that they cook through.

Eggplant with Dengaku Sauce

serves 4

4 eggplants, each about 4 ounces (120 g)

4 tablespoons sesame oil or olive oil

sauce

2 tablespoons red miso

1 tablespoon sugar

2 tablespoons saké or white wine

1 tablespoon white sesame seeds,
   ground and roasted (see page 19)

1. Cut the eggplants into long strips about ½ inch (1 cm) wide. (If the eggplant is very long, cut it in half or in thirds first.) Soak the strips in water for
   a few minutes to remove any bitterness. Drain, and dry thoroughly.

2. To make the dengaku sauce, combine the red miso, sugar, saké, and
   sesame in a small saucepan, and stir gently over low heat for 3 to 4 minutes until the mixture starts to thicken (see photo).

3. Heat a frying pan, add the sesame oil, and then add the eggplants. Fry over
   medium heat until both sides are golden brown. Alternatively, baste the
   eggplants with sesame oil and roast in the oven at 360°F (180°C) for
   5 to 6 minutes.

4. Arrange the eggplants on a serving plate, and dress with the dengaku
   sauce.

Stir the dengaku sauce over low heat.

Green Beans and Eggplant with Sesame Dressing

serves 4

5 1/2 ounces (150 g) green beans, with strings removed

3 eggplants, each about 4 ounces (120 g), sliced into 1/2-inch (1-cm) disks

3 tablespoons sesame oil

4 tablespoons saké

dressing

3 tablespoons black sesame paste

2 tablespoons sugar

2 tablespoons soy sauce

1. Boil the green beans in salted water until tender, then cut into 1 1/2-inch (3–4-cm) lengths. Soak the eggplant in water for a few minutes to remove any bitterness. Drain and dry thoroughly.

2. Heat the sesame oil in a frying pan, add the eggplant, and fry until both sides are golden brown. Add the saké to the pan, cover, and leave to steam on medium heat for 2 to 3 minutes.

3. To make the dressing, combine the black sesame paste, sugar, and soy sauce, and mix well.

4. Mix the green beans and eggplant with the sesame dressing, and arrange on a serving plate.

Steaming the eggplant after frying in sesame oil enhances the flavor.

Fried Eggplant in Sesame Sauce

serves 4

4 eggplants, each about 4 ounces (120 g), sliced into 1/2-inch (1-cm) disks

vegetable oil, for deep-frying

white sesame seeds, roasted, for garnish (see page 19)

sauce

2 tablespoons white sesame seeds, roasted and ground (see page 19)

1 tablespoon sugar

1 tablespoon soy sauce

1 teaspoon lemon juice

1 teaspoon white miso, or 1/2 teaspoon red miso

1. Soak the eggplant in water for a few minutes to remove any bitterness. Drain, dry thoroughly, and deep-fry in vegetable oil preheated to 340–360°F (170–180°C) for 2 to 3 minutes or until golden brown.

2. To make the sauce, combine the ground sesame, sugar, soy sauce, lemon juice, and miso, and mix well.

3. Arrange the eggplant on a serving plate, dress with the sauce, and sprinkle with sesame seeds.

Mushrooms with Plum Sauce

This tart plum sauce enhances the different textures and flavors of the mushrooms.

serves 4

4 tablespoons olive oil

7 ounces (200 g) eringi mushrooms, thinly sliced

2 ounces (60 g) button mushroom caps, thinly sliced

1 ounce (30 g) fresh shiitake mushroom caps, thinly sliced

1 ounce (30 g) shimeji mushrooms, separated into clusters

2 tablespoons lemon juice

umeboshi plum, minced, for garnish

white sesame seeds, roasted and ground, for garnish (see page 19)

sauce

1 block firm tofu, about 3 1/2 ounces (100 g)

3 umeboshi pickled plums, pitted

2 tablespoons mirin

1 tablespoon lemon juice

1. Wrap the tofu in a paper towel or tea towel (see page 24), place a plate on top and refrigerate for 30 minutes to remove excess moisture.

2. To make the sauce, blend the tofu, plums, mirin, and lemon juice in a food processor until smooth.

3. Heat a frying pan, add the olive oil, then add the mushrooms, and fry over medium heat for about 10 minutes. Remove from the heat and sprinkle with the 2 tablespoons of lemon juice while still hot.

4. Arrange the mushrooms on a serving plate, and top with the sauce. Garnish with minced umeboshi and ground white sesame.

Cucumber, Wakame and Peas with Vinegar-Miso Dressing

When the first southerly wind of the year arrives, wakame seaweed is dashed onto the beach near my house. When cooked, the wakame turns from brown to vibrant green and I feel that spring has arrived.

serves 4

2 Japanese cucumbers

¹/₂ teaspoon salt

¹/₃ cup (5 g) dried wakame

2 ounces (60 g) snow peas, with strings removed

roasted white sesame seeds (see page 19), for garnish

slivers of fresh ginger, for garnish, optional

finely shredded shiso leaves, for garnish, optional

dressing

3 tablespoons white miso, or 1 tablespoon red miso

1 ¹/₂ tablespoons sugar

6 tablespoons rice vinegar or any white vinegar

1. Sprinkle the cucumbers with the salt, roll (see photo), then cut into thin oval slices.

2. Soak the wakame in water for about 10 minutes until soft, drain, then plunge briefly into boiling water. Drain, and cut into bite-sized pieces.

3. Cook the snow peas in boiling water for 1 minute, plunge briefly into cold water, then cut in half on the diagonal.

4. To make the dressing, combine the miso, sugar, and vinegar, and mix well. Add the cucumber, snow peas, and wakame, toss gently, then sprinkle with roasted sesame seeds. The dish can also be garnished with finely sliced fresh ginger or shiso leaves.

Rolling the cucumbers

POTATOES
RICE
and
GRAINS

Scattered Vegetable Sushi

Sushi rice mixed with cooked vegetables, boiled shrimp, and cooked egg is a traditional festive meal in Japan, served on occasions such as the Dolls' Festival on March 3rd, and on children's birthdays. In this recipe, vegetables cooked in a sweet-and-sour sauce are added to sushi rice to make a deliciously moist dish that will have everyone asking for a second helping.

serves 4

5³⁄₄ cups (700 g) sushi rice (see page 97)

4 dried shiitake mushrooms

2¹⁄₂ cups (600 ml) water

2 ounces (60 g) burdock root

1¹⁄₄ ounces (40 g) koyadofu

3 tablespoons sugar

4 tablespoons soy sauce

4 tablespoons saké

2 ounces (60 g) carrot, peeled and sliced into ³⁄₄-inch (2-cm) matchsticks

¹⁄₄ cup (40 g) cooked soybeans

2 ounces (60 g) lotus root, peeled, quartered, and thinly sliced

1 tablespoon rice vinegar

1 tablespoon sugar mixed with 2 tablespoons rice vinegar

1³⁄₄ ounces (50 g) green beans, strings removed, and sliced into ³⁄₄-inch (2-cm) pieces on the diagonal

white sesame seeds, roasted, for garnish (see page 19)

sprigs of sansho, for garnish, optional

1. Soak the shiitake in the water for 30 minutes to reconstitute, remove the hard stems, and slice the caps thinly. Reserve the shiitake water.

2. Clean and scrape the burdock root (see page 99), slice into ³⁄₄-inch (2-cm) lengths, and immediately soak in water for 5 minutes.

3. Soak the koyadofu for 2 to 3 minutes in hot water, drain, and squeeze gently to remove excess moisture. Cut into thin slices ¹⁄₂ inch (1 cm) long.

4. In a saucepan, combine the shiitake water, sugar, soy sauce, and saké, and place over heat. Then add the shiitake, burdock root, koyadofu, carrot, and soybeans, and bring to a boil. Remove any froth from the surface. Turn the heat to low, and cook for a further 7 to 8 minutes. Turn off the heat and let stand for about 15 minutes, then drain.

5. Soak the lotus root for a few minutes in cold water with a few drops of rice vinegar to remove any astringency, then drain.

6. Put the lotus root in a saucepan with 1 tablespoon of rice vinegar and just enough water to cover. Place over medium heat, cook for 5 to 6 minutes until tender crisp, remove, drain, and soak in the sugar-and-vinegar mixture for 20 minutes. Drain.

7. Blanch the green beans in boiling salted water, then drain.

8. Gently mix all the ingredients with the sushi rice. Garnish with sesame seeds and sansho, if available.

*Nanohana (rape blossoms) also make an attractive garnish. Blanch the nanohana in boiling water, then arrange on top of the rice.

Sushi Rolls

Prepared in advance, sushi rolls are perfect for picnics or birthday celebrations. Alternatively, simply prepare a bowl of sushi rice, a plate of nori sheets, and set out various ingredients so that everyone can choose their favorite fillings and roll their own sushi.

1

makes 4 rolls

5 3/4 cups (700 g) sushi rice (see page 97)

1 1/4 ounces (40 g) carrot, peeled

1 ounce (30 g) cheese

1 ounce (30 g) dill pickle, large size

4 sheets nori seaweed, about 7 1/2 x 8 inches (19 x 21 cm) square

sweet vinegared ginger, for garnish (see page 97)

2

1. Cut the carrot, cheese, and pickle into pieces 4 inches (10 cm) long and 1/4 inch (5 mm) wide. Boil the carrot for 6 to 7 minutes until soft all the way through.

2. Lay out a sushi rolling mat (or a piece of plastic wrap), place a sheet of nori on top, shiny side down, and carefully spread the sushi rice over the nori to a thickness of about 1/2 inch (1 cm). Leave a border of about 3/4 inch (2 cm) along the edges of the nori sheet (see photo 1).

3. Make a shallow trough in the center of the rice, and place the slices of carrot, pickles and cheese in it (see photo 2).

4. From the edge closest to you, pick up the rolling mat and the nori together and roll up the sushi. Once rolled, squeeze the rolling mat firmly to shape the roll into a solid round shape (see photo 3). Press both ends to make sure that no sushi rice falls out.

3

5. Remove the rolling mat and cut into bite-sized pieces with a sharp knife (see photo 4).

6. Repeat the process until all ingredients have been used.

7. Serve with sweet vinegared ginger.

*Warm the knife in hot water for a few minutes before cutting the sushi roll.

4

Reverse Sushi Rolls with Millet

makes 4 rolls

5³⁄₄ cups (700 g) sushi rice with millet
   (see below)

¹⁄₂ Japanese cucumber

1 ounce (30 g) carrot, peeled

¹⁄₂ avocado, peeled and pitted

4 sheets nori seaweed, about 7¹⁄₂ x
   8 inches (19 x 21 cm) square

2 tablespoons white sesame seeds,
   roasted (see page 19)

1. Cut the cucumber and carrot into pieces
   4 inches (10 cm) long and ¹⁄₄ inch (5 mm) wide.
   Boil the carrot for 6 to 7 minutes until soft. Cut
   the avocado into thin slices.

2. Place a piece of plastic wrap on a rolling mat,
   sprinkle the wrap lightly with water to prevent
   the rice from sticking, and then spread the sushi
   rice on top. Cover the rice with a sheet of nori,
   then place pieces of cucumber, carrot, and avocado on top (see photo 1).

3. Roll up the mat from the edge closest to you
   (see photo 2).

4. Remove the rolling mat and plastic wrap, then
   sprinkle the rice with the sesame seeds. Cut the
   roll into bite-sized pieces (see photo 3).

5. Repeat the process until all ingredients have
   been used.

1

2

3

sushi rice with millet

1¹⁄₂ cups (320 g) uncooked rice

2 tablespoons millet

1 piece dried konbu, about 2 inches
   (5 cm) square

1⁴⁄₅ cups water (440 ml)

Place the ingredients in a saucepan, leave to soak for 30 minutes, then cook
the sushi rice in the usual way (see page 97).

*1 tablespoon of black or wild rice may be used instead of millet.

Shiitake Sushi

In Japanese this dish is known as temari sushi because the colorful, ball-shaped pieces of sushi resemble the traditional temari, a decorative cloth ball covered in colorful silk yarns in an intricate pattern.

makes 8

2 cups (240 g) sushi rice (see page 97)

8 dried shiitake mushrooms

$^4/_5$ cup (200 ml) water

1 $^1/_2$ tablespoons sugar

2 tablespoons soy sauce

finely grated yuzu rind, for garnish, optional

1. Soak the shiitake in the water for 30 minutes to reconstitute. Drain, reserving the water. Remove the shiitake stems.

2. In a saucepan, mix the shiitake water, sugar, and soy sauce, then place over low heat. Add the shiitake caps and cook for 7 to 8 minutes until the liquid evaporates.

3. Place the shiitake caps top-side down on individual pieces of plastic wrap. Divide the sushi rice into 8 portions, and place each portion on an upside-down mushroom cap. Use the plastic wrap to form each shiitake and rice portion into a ball shape (see photo).

4. Remove the plastic wrap, arrange the balls on a serving plate (see page 81), and garnish with yuzu rind.

Use the plastic wrap to shape the sushi into a ball.

Chestnut Tea Rice

In Japan, rice is often cooked with seasonal vegetables, such as bamboo shoots in the spring, or mushrooms or nuts in the fall. In this recipe, rice is cooked with chestnuts and sprinkled with aromatic green tea leaves.

serves 4

1 $\frac{1}{2}$ cups (320 g) uncooked rice

12 chestnuts, peeled

1 $\frac{4}{5}$ cups (440 ml) water

2 teaspoons soy sauce

$\frac{1}{2}$ teaspoon salt

1 heaping tablespoon sencha
   green tea leaves

1. Wash the rice (see page 97).

2. Soak the chestnuts in salted water for 30 minutes, then drain.

3. Place rice, 1 $\frac{4}{5}$ cups (440 ml) water, chestnuts, soy sauce, and salt in a saucepan, and cook in the usual way (see page 97).

4. Place a sheet of cooking paper on the bottom of a frying pan, spread the green tea leaves on top of the paper and roast over a low flame for 2 to 3 minutes. With fingertips, crumble the leaves to a fine powder, and sprinkle over the rice just before serving.

Ginger Rice

The fresh flavor of ginger is ideal with freshly cooked rice. When the president of a French champagne vineyard visited us, we served him ginger rice and Kenchin style vegetable soup (see page 15). He said it would go perfectly with a glass of bubbly!

serves 4

1 ½ cups (320 g) uncooked rice

1 ⁴/₅ cups (440 ml) water

2 pieces dried konbu, about 2 inches (5 cm) square

1 ½ tablespoons soy sauce

1 tablespoon saké

1 ounce (30 g) fresh ginger, peeled and grated

thinly sliced ginger, for garnish

1. Wash the rice (see page 97).

2. Put the rice in a saucepan, add the water, konbu, soy sauce, and saké, and mix well. Leave to soak for 30 minutes, then cook in the usual way (see page 97).

3. Squeeze the grated ginger firmly by hand over a bowl to extract the juice.

4. When the rice is cooked, remove the konbu, lightly fluff, add the ginger juice, and gently cut and mix with a spatula. Divide into serving bowls, and garnish with the thinly sliced ginger.

Fresh ginger, peeled and thinly sliced.

New Potatoes with Peanut-Miso Dressing

serves 4

serves 4

8 1/2 ounces (240 g) new potatoes, peeled and sliced into 2-inch (5-cm) matchsticks

2 ounces (60 g) carrot, peeled and sliced into 2-inch (5-cm) matchsticks

dressing

1 tablespoon red miso

2 tablespoons mirin

1 tablespoon sugar

2 tablespoons lemon juice

4 tablespoons finely crushed peanuts, sesame seeds or walnuts, or 2 tablespoons of unsweetened peanut butter

1. Bring the potatoes to a boil in a saucepan of salted water on medium heat until cooked through but still slightly hard in the middle. Drain.

2. Cook the carrot in a saucepan of water for 5 minutes on medium heat, then drain.

3. To make the dressing, combine the red miso, mirin, sugar, lemon juice, and crushed peanuts, and mix well.

4. Drain the potatoes and carrot thoroughly, arrange on a serving plate, and cover with the dressing.

Spicy Stir-Fried Potato

serves 4

14 ounces (400 g) potatoes, peeled and cut in 1/2-inch (1-cm) dice

2 tablespoons red miso

1 1/2 tablespoons sugar

2 tablespoons saké

2 tablespoons sesame oil

2 dried red chili peppers, sliced thinly

2 teaspoons soy sauce

1. Rinse the potatoes, then boil in salted water until tender crisp.

2. In a bowl, combine the red miso, sugar, and saké, and mix well.

3. Heat the sesame oil in a frying pan. Add the chili peppers and cook for 1 to 2 minutes. Add the potatoes, fry until transparent, then add the soy sauce.

4. Add the miso mixture to the frying pan, and cook over low heat for 1 to 2 minutes, stirring, until the potatoes are completely coated with the sauce.

Seaweed and Potato Patties

makes 16

4 ounces (120 g) potatoes, peeled

1 sheet of nori seaweed, about 7 ½ x 8 inches (19 x 21 cm) square

½ tablespoon sesame oil

1 tablespoon mirin mixed with 1 table-spoon soy sauce

1 teaspoon white sesame seeds, roasted, for garnish (see page 19)

shichimi pepper, for garnish, optional

1. Blend the potatoes to a rough paste in a food processor, then wrap in a paper towel to remove excess moisture.

2. Cut the nori into 16 squares and place a spoonful of potato on each.

3. Fry the potato-and-nori squares in the sesame oil, nori side up, until the potato is golden brown. Then briefly fry the nori side.

4. Arrange on a serving plate, drizzled with the mirin-and-soy-sauce mixture, and garnished with sesame and shichimi.

Fried Potato Cakes

makes about 18

14 ounces (400 g) potatoes, peeled and sliced into thin matchsticks

⅔ cup (80 g) all-purpose flour

⅓ cup (80 ml) water

1 teaspoon salt

2 tablespoons finely chopped parsley

¼ cup (40 g) cooked soybeans

2 teaspoons black sesame seeds, roasted (see page 19)

4 tablespoons sesame oil

1. Boil the potatoes for 2 minutes.

2. In a bowl, combine the flour and water, then add the potatoes, salt, parsley, soybeans, and sesame seeds. Mix well.

3. Heat a frying pan, then add the sesame oil. When the oil is hot, pour small amounts of potato mixture into the frying pan to form cakes about 3 inches (8 cm) in diameter. Cook on medium heat for about 10 minutes, turning until both sides are golden brown and crispy. Repeat this process until all the potato mixture has been used.

Zuridashi Udon

This udon noodle dish is a favorite of novice Zen monks. The noodles are cooked in a huge saucepan, enough for thirty or forty people. The name is derived from the way the monks take the noodles from the saucepan—*zuridashi* or sliding them over the edge of the pot. Various condiments can be used to flavor the noodles.

serves 4

14 ounces (400 g) dried udon noodles

condiments

4 tablespoons white sesame seeds, roasted and ground (see page 19)

3 1/2 ounces (100 g) daikon radish, peeled and grated

1 sheet nori seaweed, cut into thin strips

shichimi pepper

2 tablespoons finely grated yuzu rind

2 tablespoons finely grated fresh ginger

2 tablespoons chopped mitsuba sprigs

4 tablespoons soy sauce

1. Fill a saucepan with ample water, bring to a boil, add the udon, and cook for about 20 minutes, or until the noodles are soft. Drain the noodles and place in a bowl. Reserve the cooking liquid.

2. Place the condiments (sesame, daikon, nori, shichimi, yuzu, ginger, mitsuba) in small serving dishes. Soy sauce and the water used to cook the udon can also be used as condiments to sprinkle over the noodles.

3. Serve the udon noodles in individual bowls, and eat while still piping hot, sprinkled with your favorite condiments.

*You can place the saucepan of noodles on the table and everyone can serve themselves.

Buckwheat Crepes

Buckwheat flour is most commonly eaten in the form of soba noodles, but it is also delicious when used to make this semi-sweet healthy snack.

serves 4

1 1/4 cups (200 g) buckwheat flour

1 2/3 cups (400 ml) water

1 teaspoon salt

1 tablespoon finely ground walnuts

1 tablespoon sliced almonds

2 teaspoons black sesame seeds, roasted (see page 19)

3 tablespoons raisins

4 tablespoons olive oil

seasonal vegetables

sauce

2 tablespoons red miso

3 tablespoons red wine

2 tablespoons maple syrup

2 tablespoons peanut butter, unsweetened type

1. In a bowl, mix all the sauce ingredients together.

2. To make the batter, combine the flour, water and salt, then add the walnuts, sliced almonds, sesame seeds and raisins. Mix well.

3. Heat a frying pan, and add the olive oil. When the oil is hot, pour in the batter so that it covers the base of the pan in a thin layer. Cook on medium heat until both sides are golden brown. Repeat this process until all the batter has been used.

4. Arrange the crepes on individual serving plates while still hot, and dress with the sauce. Serve with seasonal vegetables.

DESSERTS

Soymilk Jelly with Strawberry Sauce

This recipe uses agar-agar, a form of gelatin derived from seaweed, which is full of healthy fiber. It is often used in desserts.

serves 8	sauce
4 teaspoons agar-agar powder	3 1/2 ounces (100 g) strawberries
3 1/3 cups (800 ml) soymilk	2 tablespoons lemon juice
4 tablespoons maple syrup	2 tablespoons maple syrup

1. To make the sauce, place the strawberries in a small saucepan, and mash and stir over low heat for 5 to 6 minutes. Remove from the heat and leave to cool. Blend the strawberries, lemon juice, and maple syrup in a food processor.

2. Combine the agar-agar and soymilk in a saucepan, and mix well. When the agar-agar is completely dissolved, mix in the maple syrup. Place over heat, bring to a boil, then remove from the heat.

3. When the soymilk has cooled, pour into cups or molds, and refrigerate until set.

4. Serve the jellies in individual dishes, dressed with the sauce.

Blackened Dried Figs

Served with ginger tea (a few drops of freshly squeezed ginger in hot water, with sugar to taste), this dessert is a real pick-me-up.

serves 4

16 dried figs
3 tablespoons raw sugar
1 1/4 cups (300 ml) water

1. Rinse the dried figs and leave to soak in water for 10 minutes.

2. Place the figs, sugar and the 1 1/4 cups (300 ml) of water in a saucepan, and simmer for about 20 minutes on low heat. Leave to cool before serving.

Soymilk Mousse with Blueberry Sauce

Blueberry sauce adds sweetness to this smooth, tasty dessert.

serves 4

2 tablespoons plain yogurt, unsweet-
    ened type

2 tablespoons lemon juice

2/5 cup (100 ml) soymilk

1 block firm tofu, about 7 ounces
    (200 g), undrained

5 ounces (140 g) banana, peeled

sauce

1 3/4 ounces (50 g) dried blueberries

4/5 cup (200 ml) soymilk

2 tablespoons lemon juice

2 tablespoons maple syrup

1. In a food processor, blend the yogurt, lemon juice, soymilk, tofu, and banana for 2 to 3 minutes, until thick and smooth.

2. To make the sauce, combine the blueberries, soymilk, lemon juice, and maple syrup in a saucepan, bring to a boil, then cook on low heat for about 30 minutes.

3. Serve the mousse in individual dishes, topped with the sauce.

Pears in Wine

Pears are cooked in wine, chilled and served with yogurt. Apples, figs or plums can also be used.

serves 4

2 1/2 cups (600 ml) red wine

3 tablespoons maple syrup

3 tablespoons lemon juice

2 pears, peeled and cut into
    bite-sized pieces

4 tablespoons plain yogurt, unsweet-
    ened type

mint leaves, for garnish, optional

1. In a saucepan, combine the red wine, maple syrup, and lemon juice. Add the pears and cook on low heat for 10 to 12 minutes until transparent. Remove from the heat, let cool to room temperature, then refrigerate for 30 minutes.

2. Serve the pears and sauce in individual bowls, garnished with yogurt and mint leaves.

Banana Tempura

serves 4

4 bananas, peeled and cut diagonally
  into ¾-inch (2-cm) slices

vegetable oil, for deep-frying

dash powdered green tea or powdered cinnamon

batter

½ cup (60 g) all-purpose flour

⅓ cup (80 ml) water

½ teaspoon salt

2 teaspoons white sesame seeds,
  roasted (see page 19)

1. To make the batter, combine the flour, water, salt and sesame seeds, and mix well.

2. Dip the banana slices in the batter, then deep-fry in vegetable oil preheated to 340°F (170°C) until they turn golden brown. Bananas burn easily, so be careful not to overcook.

3. Divide the fried banana slices between individual serving dishes, and dust with powdered green tea using a tea-strainer.

Kiwi Fruit with Mashed Potato

makes 8

4 kiwi fruits, peeled, quartered, and
  thinly sliced

2 tablespoons honey or maple syrup

7 ounces (200 g) potato, peeled and
  sliced into ½-inch (1-cm) rounds

½ teaspoon salt

1. Mix the kiwi fruit with the honey.

2. Boil the potato on medium heat in just enough salted water to cover for about 10 minutes, or until soft. Drain any excess liquid, return to the heat, and mash until moist but not too dry. Leave to cool.

3. Divide the mashed potato into 8 portions. Place each portion on a sheet of plastic wrap. Remove the kiwi slices from the honey and distribute evenly on top of the mashed potato portions. Use the plastic wrap to cover each kiwi-topped potato portion and shape into a ball.

4. Remove the plastic wrap and arrange the balls on serving plates.

BASIC PREPARATION TECHNIQUES

How to Wash Rice

1. Put the rice in a bowl, add ample water, stir briefly by hand, and discard the cloudy water.

2. Repeat this process 3 or 4 times until the water is almost clear. Drain in a sieve.

How to Cook Rice

makes 5¾ cups (700 g)

1½ cups (320 g) rice
1⅘ cups (440 ml) water

1. Place the rice and water in a saucepan, and leave to soak for 30 minutes.

2. Cook on high for 5 to 6 minutes, then turn the heat to low and cook for a further 14 to 15 minutes. When the rice stops bubbling and starts to make a popping sound, turn the heat to high for 1 or 2 seconds then remove from the heat. Leave to steam, covered with a lid, for 10 minutes. If the rice is still a little hard, sprinkle with 2 tablespoons of saké, cover with a lid and leave to steam for a further 5 to 6 minutes.

*If using an automatic rice cooker, wash the rice in the usual way, then follow the instruction manual.

Wash the rice in ample water, stirring briefly by hand.

How to Make Sushi Rice

makes 5¾ cups (700 g)

1½ cups (320 g) uncooked rice
1 piece dried konbu, about 2 inches (5 cm) square
1⅘ cups (440 ml) water

vinegar dressing

¼ cup (60 ml) rice vinegar
2 tablespoons sugar
1 teaspoon salt

1. Wash the rice, following the instructions on this page, drain in a sieve, and leave for 30 minutes. Cook the rice, following the instructions on this page, with the konbu added to the cooking water.

2. In a small saucepan, stir the vinegar, sugar, and salt over low heat, until the sugar and salt have dissolved.

3. When the rice is cooked, place in a bowl, remove the konbu, and gradually mix in the vinegar dressing using cutting motions with a spatula.

Sweet Vinegared Ginger

1¾ ounces (50 g) fresh ginger, peeled and thinly sliced
dash salt
⅕ cup (50 ml) rice vinegar
1 teaspoon sugar

1. Boil the ginger in water for 2 to 3 minutes, then drain, and sprinkle lightly with salt.

2. In a saucepan, heat the rice vinegar and sugar until the sugar dissolves. Turn off the heat and leave to cool.

3. Add the salted ginger to the vinegar-and-sugar mixture, and leave to soak for 10 minutes before using.

How to Make Stock

Konbu stock and shiitake stock are two of the most commonly used in temple cuisine, and are easy to make. Ready-made vegan stock (also known as vegan *dashi*) can also be found in Asian supermarkets and natural food stores.

konbu stock

1 2/3 cups (400 ml) water

1 piece dried konbu, 4 inches (10 cm) square

1. The white powder on the surface of dried konbu adds to the flavor, so do not wash the konbu before use, simply lightly wipe with a damp cloth.

2. Place the water and the konbu in a saucepan, and leave to soak for 2 or 3 hours.

3. Place the saucepan over medium heat. Just before the water boils, remove the konbu. Use the konbu-flavored water as stock.

Making konbu stock

shiitake stock

2 or 3 dried shiitake mushrooms

1 2/3 cups (400 ml) water

1. Rinse the shiitake.

2. Soak the shiitake in the water for 2 to 3 hours, then remove. Use the shiitake-flavored water as stock.

*The reconstituted shiitake can be used in many other recipes.

GLOSSARY

Most of these ingredients are generally available from Asian supermarkets, natural food stores and online shopping sites.

Agar-Agar Powder

Agar-agar powder is made from seaweed, and has gelatin-like thickening properties. It is used in many jellied dishes and Japanese sweets. Rich in dietary fiber yet low in calories, it is excellent as a diet food. A teaspoon of agar-agar powder added to rice while cooking will make the rice shine beautifully. Agar-agar can also be found in stick or filament form.

Burdock Root

Burdock root is about 1 inch (2–3 cm) in diameter and 15–20 inches (40–50 cm) long. It has a firm texture and distinctive aroma, and is rich in dietary fiber. Before cooking, scrub thoroughly and scrape off the skin with the back of a kitchen knife. Scraping rather than peeling retains more of the flavor. Slice, and soak in water for 5 minutes to remove any bitterness.

*Choose shorter, firm roots

*Store in the refrigerator wrapped in wet kitchen paper.

Daikon Radish

Daikon is a winter root vegetable, about 16 inches (40 cm) long, and the most commonly grown and popularly used vegetable in Japan. It is eaten raw in salads, cooked in stews, or pickled. Full of vitamin C and other nutrients, it is also good for the digestion. The leaves can be blanched, fried in sesame oil, and seasoned with salt and soy sauce. Daikon is also preserved with salt and rice bran to make a pickle known as takuan.

*Choose a daikon that is firm and glossy.

*If you purchase a whole daikon, cut off the leaves, wrap the radish in paper and refrigerate. Wrap the leaves in wet paper, place in a plastic bag and refrigerate.

Edamame Beans

Edamame beans are soybeans harvested while still green. They are in season from summer to early fall in Japan, and are rich in protein and vitamin C. After boiling in their pods they can be sprinkled with salt and eaten as a snack, or blended to a smooth paste for soup.

*Edamame beans can be bought fresh or frozen.

*Boiled edamame beans will keep refrigerated for a few days. They can also be frozen.

Eggplant

In Japan, eggplants can be long, round, or small, but the most commonly available is about 6 inches (15 cm) long. Japanese eggplants have soft skin, a sweet, delicate flavor, and are used in a wide range of dishes, such as pickles, tempura, and stews. Eggplants have a cooling effect on the body in summer.

*Choose glossy eggplants with burrs on the cap and a freshly cut stalk.

*If chilled too much, eggplants lose their flavor, so wrap in newspaper and place inside a plastic bag before refrigerating.

Enoki Mushrooms

Milky white mushrooms about 4 inches (10 cm) long, enoki are crispy and firm. They are often found in winter hot pots, or blanched and served with a dressing. They are also edible raw. Cut off the spongy root about 1 inch (2–3 cm) from the bottom before using.

*Choose enoki that are firm and white with an elastic texture.

*To store, cover with plastic wrap and refrigerate.

Eringi Mushrooms

Eringi are plump, milky white mushrooms with a crunchy texture and a delicate flavor.

*Choose eringi that are firm and white with an elastic texture.

*To store, cover with plastic wrap and refrigerate.

Green Tea

Green tea comes in many varieties. Sencha is a leaf tea, used for everyday tea drinking. Powdered tea, known as matcha, is used in the tea ceremony, and can also be mixed with salt as a seasoning for tempura, blended with soymilk, or used in cakes and sweets. Green tea is rich in vitamin C.

*Store in an airtight container.

Hijiki

Hijiki seaweed is usually sold dried. To use, rinse gently in a sieve to remove any dirt, then soak in water to reconstitute. Hijiki can be combined with other vegetables in salads or fried dishes, or simply boiled and served with a dressing. It is rich in iron, calcium, potassium and dietary fiber.

*Store dried hijiki in an airtight container.

Japanese Cucumber

The Japanese cucumber is about 8 inches (20 cm) long and 1 inch (2–3 cm) in diameter. Cucumbers are eaten raw in salads, or salted and pickled. A member of the melon family, cucumber has a cooling effect on the body and expels excess heat.

*In the store, choose fresh cucumbers with spiny skins.

Kabu Turnip

In season from fall to winter, kabu turnips are white or red, and 1½–3 inches (4–8 cm) in diameter. The white variety is more commonly used in Japan. Often pickled, or eaten in stews and soups, kabu contain vitamin C and are good for the digestion.

*Select kabu which are firm and round.

*To store, cut off the leaves, wrap the turnip in paper and refrigerate. Wrap the leaves in wet paper, place in a plastic bag, and refrigerate.

Karashi Mustard

Karashi is available in powdered or paste forms. If using powder, mix a small amount with warm water, cover the bowl with plastic wrap and leave for 10 minutes. Karashi can be eaten with salads and stews, and stimulates the appetite.

*Store powdered karashi in an airtight container. Once mixed with water, karashi cannot be stored, as it loses its flavor.

Konbu

Konbu is a dried seaweed used to make stock in temple cuisine (see page 98). It varies in width from 2–12 inches (5–30 cm) and can grow up to 20 yards (18 meters) long. Konbu is rich in amino acids, dietary fiber, and calcium.

*Choose konbu that is almost black in color, thick, and has a fine white powder on the surface.

*Store dried konbu in an airtight container.

Konnyaku

Konnyaku is a gelatinous paste made from the tuberous root known as devil's tongue. This paste is formed into blocks or noodles. Konnyaku has little taste and is enjoyed mainly for its texture. A foodstuff with no calories, it is popular as a diet food. Rinse and boil for 2 to 3 minutes before using. Konnyaku can be served dengaku style, with a miso topping, or used in soups and stews.

*Once the packet has been opened, store in the refrigerator in ample water. The water should be changed daily.

Koyadofu

Koyadofu is freeze-dried tofu. It takes its name from Mount Koya, the place of the temple where it is said to have been invented. Soak in water for 2 to 3 minutes

to reconstitute, then squeeze gently to remove excess moisture before using. Koyadofu is used in stews and fried dishes, or flavored with a salty-sweet sauce and used in sushi rolls.

*Store in a sealed bag in a dry place.

Lotus Root

The root of the lotus plant has crunchy, off-white flesh, and holes which run the length of the tuber. Before use, wash thoroughly to remove any mud from the holes, then pare off the skin. After cutting, soak in water with a few drops of vinegar. Lotus root is often pickled or used in fried or stewed dishes. It is rich in vitamin C and dietary fiber.

*Choose roots with no cuts in the skin, and firm, grayish-white or cream-colored flesh. Check the inside surfaces of the air holes which run through the root. If these surfaces are dark, the lotus root is not fresh.

*To store, wrap in damp newspaper and refrigerate.

Millet

A small yellow grain of the rice family, millet has been grown in Japan for centuries. Rich in dietary fiber, it has recently been rediscovered as a health food. One easy-to-digest cooking method is to boil 1 tablespoon of millet with ¾ cup (160 g) of rice.

Mirin

Mirin is a liqueur used for cooking, made from a fermented mixture of distilled rice spirits, rice malt and glutinous rice. Mirin imparts a refined sweetness, flavor and aroma to a dish, and gives a shiny glaze to ingredients, as well as preventing them from disintegrating when boiled. It is an essential seasoning in temple cuisine. When mirin is not available, use sugar, and halve the quantity by volume.

Miso

Miso is a paste of fermented soybeans widely used in Japanese cuisine as a seasoning for soups or stews, or mixed with vegetables as a snack or side dish. Red and white miso are the two main types available. White miso is often used in dressings, whereas the stronger flavor of red miso is good in soups.

*Store in an airtight container in the refrigerator.

Mitsuba

Mitsuba is a savory herb with a particularly

strong aroma in spring. It is often used as a garnish for vegetables and soups. It contains carotene, calcium, and vitamin C.

*Store in damp paper in a polythene bag and refrigerate.

Nagaimo Yam

Nagaimo is one of the many varieties of Japanese yam, with a cylindrical shape, about 3 inches (7–8 cm) in diameter. It has a delicious crunchy texture when grated or finely sliced and sprinkled with a vinegar and soy sauce dressing.

*Choose yams with unblemished skin.

*To store, wrap in damp newspaper and refrigerate. Once peeled, do not keep, as the white flesh turns an unappealing gray color.

Natto

Natto is the name for soybeans that have been steamed and fermented, a process which creates its characteristic viscous consistency. Before using, mix well until sticky, add soy sauce, and mix again.

*Natto is usually sold in small plastic cartons.

*Natto can be frozen.

Nori Seaweed

Nori seaweed is dried into thin, flat sheets and usually sold in packs of ten. Rich in protein and vitamin A, it is most commonly used as the wrapping for sushi rolls.

*Choose nori that is black, glossy and thick.

*Once opened, store in an airtight container.

Pickled Plum Paste

Pickled plum paste is available ready-made in jars from Asian stores. (See also Umeboshi Pickled Plum)

Pumpkin

Japanese pumpkin comes in several varieties. In temple cuisine, the small kikuza or kuro-kawa pumpkin is often used for its rich yellow flesh and mild taste. The outer skin is ridged, and dark green-black. Pumpkin contains carbohydrates, carotene, and vitamins B1, B2, and C.

*To store leftover, uncooked pumpkin, remove the seeds and stringy fibers, cover the cut edges with plastic wrap, and refrigerate.

Raw Sugar

Raw sugar is made from the boiled juice of sugar cane. It has a distinctive flavor and can be used in stews, or made into syrup for use in confectionery. If you feel a cold coming on, some raw sugar dissolved in hot water with ginger juice is recommended. Raw sugar is rich in calcium and iron, and also contains vitamins B1 and B2.

Rice

Rice in Japan is the short-grain Japonica variety, a sweet and sticky type. Seihakumai (polished white rice with all the bran layers removed) is used for sushi. When cooking polished rice, rinse first and then leave to soak for 30 minutes. If using brown rice, soak for at least an hour before cooking, using 20 percent more water than rice. Brown rice contains more vitamin B1, calcium, dietary fiber, and iron than polished rice.

*Store in a sealed container out of direct sunlight.

Rice Vinegar

Rice vinegar is distilled vinegar made from rice and saké lees. It has a mild taste, and is the highest quality grain vinegar. It is ideal for sushi and vinegared dishes. It has an antiseptic effect, and is indispensable for fresh food preservation and the prevention of food poisoning.

Saké

Saké is wine made from rice. Although Buddhist monks avoid alcohol, saké is often used as a seasoning in cooking, or for medicinal purposes. A little saké is often said to be "the best of all medicines" because it stimulates the circulation, and relieves stress and insomnia. When cooked rice seems a little too firm, 1 or 2 tablespoons of saké will soften it (see page 97).

Sansho (Japanese Pepper)

Sansho has a refreshingly sharp fragrance and is usually sold ground. Sansho sprigs are also used as an edible garnish.

*To store sansho sprigs, wrap in paper, place in a plastic bag, and refrigerate.

Sesame Oil

Derived from ground sesame seeds, sesame oil adds fragrance to dishes. Add a little to salad dressings or to cooking oil for tempura

Sesame Paste

Sesame paste can be bought ready-made in Asian supermarkets.

Sesame Seeds

Sesame seeds are rich in protein, calcium, and vitamin B1. Both black and white sesame seeds are widely used in Japanese cuisine. Raw seeds should be roasted before using (see page 19).

*Store in an airtight container.

Shichimi Pepper

Shichimi pepper contains seven spices, which vary slightly from manufacturer to manufacturer. First created in Tokyo in 1625, one of the earliest recipes used raw cayenne peppers, roasted cayenne peppers, hemp seeds, black sesame seeds, poppy seeds, sansho and orange rind. Shichimi pepper is often used to flavor noodle dishes or stews.

Shiitake Mushrooms

Shiitake are grown from spores inoculated on beech trees and are abundant in spring and fall. They can be eaten grilled, or used in salads and deep-fried dishes. Low in calories, they are ideal as a diet food. Dried shiitake are very important in temple cuisine for stocks and boiled dishes. Shiitake are rich in dietary fiber and vitamins B1 and B2.

*Two types of dried shiitake are available in stores: the thick-capped donko shiitake

have more flavor than the flat-capped ko-shin shiitake.

*Keep dried shiitake in an airtight container.

*When buying fresh shiitake, choose mushrooms whose caps are white underneath.

*Keep fresh shiitake in the refrigerator wrapped in paper. Do not keep in a polythene bag as this will make the mushrooms slimy.

Shimeji Mushrooms

In season from fall to winter, shimeji mushrooms have gray caps and short, fat stems. They are often used in hot pots and mixed rice dishes. In the fall, wild shimeji can be found in small numbers in broadleaf forests. The flavor disappears if they are washed too well before use. Cut off the spongy part of the stem about 1 inch (2–3 cm) from the bottom, and quickly rinse. Shimeji are rich in vitamin B2, which is said to be good for the complexion.

*Choose shimeji which are plump, and firm to the touch.

*Wrap in paper and keep in the refrigerator.

Shiso (Perilla)

In season from early summer to fall, shiso is a fragrant herb easily grown in the garden or a planter. Its remarkable fragrance makes it essential as a garnish for sashimi or soups. Shiso is rich in vitamins A and C, contains calcium, and stimulates the appetite.

*To store, wrap in damp paper and refrigerate.

Soy Sauce

An essential item in Japanese cuisine, soy sauce is made from soybeans, wheat, salt, and water. It can be added to soups and stews, or served in a small saucer as a dip for sashimi. Different types of soy sauce are available, but koikuchi, or regular strong soy sauce is used in the recipes in this book.

*Soy sauce keeps best when refrigerated, although it can be stored at room temperature.

Soybeans

The soybean is the raw ingredient for tofu, natto, soy sauce, miso and soymilk. Soy-

beans contain protein, fat, glucose, B group vitamins, vitamin E, calcium, iron, and potassium. Dried soybeans should be soaked overnight then boiled for about 2 hours on low heat. Canned, ready-cooked soybeans can be found in natural food stores.

Sukikonbu

Sukikonbu is konbu seaweed sliced into strips and dried into easy-to-use sheets. Reconstitute before using by soaking in cold water for 10 minutes. Sukikonbu can be used in stews, soups and salads. It is rich in dietary fiber, vitamins, and minerals.

*Packs of sukikonbu sheets can be found in Asian supermarkets.

Sweet Potato

In Japan, sweet potatoes are usually purplish red on the outside with sweet yellow flesh. Sweet potato retains its high vitamin C and fiber content even after cooking. It is used in stews and tempura. The Japanese variety is sweet enough to be used in cakes.

*Wrap in damp newspaper and store in a dark, airy place.

Taro

An egg-shaped potato with a sticky texture, taro is a low-calorie member of the potato family, full of dietary fiber. Before boiling, rub with salt, and rinse to remove any bitterness. Because the main tuber is surrounded by five or six baby tubers, taro is used as an ingredient in New Year soup (zoni) to pray for fertility. It is often served in miso soup, or with a dengaku-style miso topping.

*Wrap in damp newspaper and store out of direct sunlight.

Tofu

Invented in China and brought to Japan around a thousand years ago, tofu is a high-protein food made from soybeans. There are two types: firm tofu, which has had moisture extracted during production, and silken tofu with the moisture retained. Tofu can be cut into small pieces and served with vegetables in a salad, or used in stews and fried dishes.

*After the pack has been opened, tofu should be kept in the refrigerator in a container of water, and used within 2 days. The water should be changed daily. Firm tofu can be frozen but silken tofu cannot.

When defrosted tofu is boiled, it acquires a delicious texture.

Udon Noodles

Udon noodles are made from wheat flour and are usually sold dried. They can be found in soup topped with tempura, or served chilled with grated daikon and other condiments. They are often added to winter hot pots.

Umeboshi Pickled Plum

Plums are picked in June and salted, then dried in the sun for three days and nights in the heat of summer. Pickled plums have an antiseptic effect, so it is good to pop one in a lunch box in the summer when food spoils easily. Pickled plum flesh can be minced, mixed with mirin and used as a dip for vegetables, or finely chopped and added to other dressings.

*Store in a jar out of direct sunlight at room temperature.

Usu-age Tofu

Usu-age refers to thin slices of deep-fried tofu. These can be grilled and eaten plain, stir-fried with other ingredients, or added to miso soup. Usu-age can also be cooked in a salty-sweet broth and stuffed with rice to make the sushi known as inarizushi. Blanch in boiling water before using to remove the slightly oily aroma.

*Keep in the refrigerator. Usu-age can also be frozen.

Wakame Seaweed

Wakame is usually available boiled and dried, but sometimes it can be found salted. Dried wakame should be soaked in cold water for 10 minutes before using. It is rich in vitamins, iron, phosphorus and calcium, and has no calories.

*Store dried wakame in an airtight container, and salted wakame in the refrigerator.

Wasabi

Wasabi is a savory herb with a pungent aroma and flavor which grows near clear mountain springs or streams. The fresh root can be peeled and grated, but it is usually sold in paste form in a tube. It has a strong antibacterial function and is always served with sashimi. It is also used to season noodle dishes. The buds and leaves of wasabi can be blanched and served in salads.

*To store fresh wasabi, wrap in damp paper, cover with plastic wrap, then refrigerate.

Yuba

A thin skin that forms on the surface of boiled soymilk, yuba is a high-protein food generally sold in dried sheets. It can be used in soups and it can also be deep-fried. Soften before using by wrapping in a damp cloth until moist.

*Keep in a sealed container in a dry place.

Yuzu

Yuzu is a citrus fruit with a fresh aroma, about 2–3 inches (5–8 cm) in diameter. In season from late fall to winter, its fragrance is closely associated with the cold months in Japan. The fruit is not edible, but the rind can be grated for zest, or sliced and added to soups, salads and hot pots to provide fragrance. Yuzu juice can be used in dressings, or added to vinegar for sushi rice. When yuzu is not available, lemon or lime can be substituted.

*Wrap in damp newspaper and refrigerate. Yuzu rind can be stored in the freezer.

INDEX

CREDITS

Tableware loaned by Wasalaby, 2-9-19 Jiyugaoka, Meguro-ku, Tokyo, 152-0035. Tel: 03-3717-
    9191 Fax: 03-3717-9200. The work of the following artisans is featured:
  Taizo Kuroda, page 1 (chopstick rest), 2–3, 13 (chopstick rest), 14 (bowl), 16–17 (bowls),
    18 (bowl), 29, 32–33, 34–35, 40, 44, 45, 52, 57, 58 (chopstick rest), 63, 79 (chopstick rest),
    84 (chopstick rest).
  Yutaka Hanaoka, page 27, 31, 49, 50–51, 56, 64, 68–69, 72–73, 74–75, 90, 94 (bottom).
  Akito Akagi, page 1 (bowls), 11 (bowl), 13 (bowl), 21 (soup bowl), 46–47, 58–59 (plates),
    60 (bowl), 61, 79 (rice bowl), 84–85 (rice bowls), 86–87, 89 (bowl), 94 (top bowl), 95 (bot-
    tom), 96 (bottom).
  Ryuji Mitani, page 16 (spoons), 18 (spoon) 21 (small dish and spoon), 24–25, 43, 60 (spoon),
    67 (spoons), 70, 79 (small dish), 80–81, 84 (small bowl), 89 (condiment dish), 94 (spoon),
    95 (spoon), 96 (top).
  Yoshihiko Takahashi, page 28, 36, 67 (glasses), 95 (top bowl).

Dried ingredients from Sanada Ltd., 2–21–13 Omiya-dori, Moriguchi-shi, Osaka 570–0033. Tel:
    06–6996–7222 Fax: 06–6997–5116.

料理セッティング	石井久美子
食材イラストレーション	鈴木淳子
AD & DTP	講談社インターナショナル　デザイン室
和紙提供	越後門出和紙

（英文版）家庭で楽しむ精進料理

2005年8月29日　第1刷発行

著　者	藤井まり
撮　影	浜村多恵
翻　訳	リチャード・ジェフリー
発行者	富田 充
発行所	講談社インターナショナル株式会社
	〒112-8652　東京都文京区音羽 1-17-14
	電話　03-3944-6493（編集部）
	03-3944-6492（営業部・業務部）
	ホームページ　www.kodansha-intl.com
印刷・製本所	大日本印刷株式会社